# DEDICATION

This book is dedicated to my wonderful wife, Janine, who is a lifelong fan of Kirk Douglas and without whose suggestion this book would probably never have happened.

# THE VERY BEST OF KIRK DOUGLAS

## THOUGHTS OF A HOLLYWOOD LEGEND

DAVID GRAHAM

Copyright © 2014 David Graham

All rights reserved.

ISBN: 1512253871
ISBN-13: 9781512253870

# CONTENTS

| | | |
|---|---|---|
| 1 | Introduction | 1 |
| 2 | About Himself and his Family | 3 |
| 3 | About Religion | 11 |
| 4 | About his Career and Acting in General | 15 |
| 5 | About Other Celebrities | 23 |
| 6 | General Philosophy and Humour | 29 |
| 7 | An Open Letter to the Youth of America | 35 |

# ACKNOWLEDGMENTS

All quotes within this book are in the words of Kirk Douglas. Although every effort has been taken to ensure the accuracy of all text, the author apologises in the event of any mistakes.

# 1 INTRODUCTION

Kirk Douglas – undoubtedly one of the finest and most admired actors ever to grace the silver screen.

Although naturally shy, Douglas overcame his self-perceived limitations to become one of the biggest names in Hollywood throughout the 50s and 60s, his roles ultimately evolving to earn him the 'tough guy' image he was perhaps most famous for.

Douglas is more than just an admired actor, however; he is a well-respected personality who has regularly offered honest opinions on a vast number of topics. He is also renowned for his respect for listening to the views of others, including those with whom his politics differ significantly.

Being myself a big fan of movies from the 'golden' era of Hollywood, I have always followed Douglas with keen interest and have nothing but sincere admiration for his honest nature and refreshing views on life.

In this book I've brought together some of the finest and

most interesting quotes from one of the world's finest actors in the history of the big screen.

# 2 ABOUT HIMSELF AND HIS FAMILY

I guess I was a bad boy... Yes, yes, I've had lots of women in my life.

\*

You know, sometimes an interviewer will look at me and say - you're bright! They're actually surprised I might be bright.

\*

Fifteen years ago, I suffered a stroke, which caused me to lose my speech. Now, what does an actor who can't talk do? Wait for silent pictures to come back? I work with a speech therapist twice a week.

*

I came from abject poverty. There was nowhere to go but up.

*

I want my sons to surpass me, because that's a form of immortality.

*

My mother, we were a very poor family. When I was a kid,

we would be in our little room, and there would be a knock on the door almost every night with a hobo begging for food. Even though we didn't even have enough to eat, my mother always found something to give them.

\*

I have one computer that my wife gave me. All I know how to do, and I do it every day, is play Spider Solitaire. And I don't have a cell phone.

\*

All my life, I have taken inventory at intervals. For example, when I became a movie actor and suddenly I had to deal with fame, money and playing so many roles, I lost myself. I said, 'Who am I?' And I wrote my first book to deal with that, 'The Ragman's Son.'

\*

# DAVID GRAHAM

If I thought a man had never committed a sin in his life, I don't think I'd want to talk with him. A man with flaws is more interesting.

\*

I have always told my sons that they didn't have my advantages of being born into abject poverty.

\*

Listen - pacemaker, crash, stroke. What does it mean? God doesn't want me now. That's all.

\*

## THE VERY BEST OF KIRK DOUGLAS

I know Italians and I like them. A lot of my father's best friends were Italians.

\*

I was living in a terrible time when people were being accused of being communists, and they attacked the movie industry, especially the writers. People couldn't work if they were on the blacklist. The studios banned them. It was the most onerous period in movie history. I don't think we have ever had a period so dark as that.

\*

When you have a stroke, you must talk slowly to be understood, and I've discovered that when I talk slowly, people listen. They think I'm going to say something important!

\*

## DAVID GRAHAM

My kids never had the advantage I had. I was born poor.

\*

What would my parents think about America if they arrived here today? Would they even want to come? I wonder.

\*

Too often, I have not been what I wanted to be; I've succumbed to pressures. Yes, I have. The things I've done that I liked, I've always done against advice.

\*

If I have to speak in public, I am terrified.

\*

You see, when a person becomes disabled, often their family starts thinking, "Oh dear, don't move, let me get that for you". Once I told my wife that I thought I wanted breakfast in bed the next morning, she said the old joke, "If you want breakfast in bed, sleep in the kitchen."

\*

Age is in the mind. I've survived a helicopter crash and back surgery. I have a pacemaker. I had a stroke that almost made me commit suicide. But I tell myself, "I have to continue growing and functioning. That's the only antidote for age.

\*

God bless Dad, he came to every one of my shows. I was bad, and I had horrible stage fright. My dad was so relieved - he'd say, 'You were terrible; this kid is not going to be an actor.' Finally, I did a play and he said, 'Son - you were really good.'

\*

You know, I've often thought if I were much older, I might not have done that; as you get older, you get more conservative, but I was still young enough to be a little bit impulsive. What got me was the hypocrisy.

\*

It seems as if only now I really know who I am. My strengths, my weaknesses, my jealousies; it's as if all of it has been boiling in a pot for all these years, and as it boils, it evaporates into steam, and all that's left in the pot in the end is your essence, the stuff you started out with in the very beginning.

# 3 ABOUT RELIGION

I studied Judaism a lot. I studied religion in general, and I have never imposed my Judaism on my kids. They are what they want to be. I think... you must care for others. That's the correct religion, I think.

\*

My four sons all knew I was a Jew, but they were allowed to be whatever they wanted to be. The only thing important to me was that they be good people who help other people, because all religion should try to make you a better person and a more caring person. Whenever religion does that for you, it's a good religion.

## DAVID GRAHAM

\*

There's too much religion. I think religion has caused so much catastrophe in the world.

\*

I was not a very good Jew. I never practised what Judaism tells you to do, to teach your kids all about Judaism.

\*

I have studied religion, and I have concluded that there is some power. We don't understand it.

\*

I think Orthodox, Hasidic Jews are terrible.

*

Every religion has some part of it that doesn't fucking work.

# 4 ABOUT HIS CAREER AND ACTING IN GENERAL

I've made a career of playing sons of bitches.

\*

I'm an actor; I have made my living by acting, and I almost think I owe it to the public to express my feelings and not as a character on a screen but as myself.

\*

Now, what does an actor who can't talk do? Wait for silent pictures to come back?

\*

I don't need a critic to tell me I'm an actor. I make my own way. Nobody's my boss. Nobody's ever been my boss.

\*

Being second generation in Hollywood is complicated: Success is expected, and yet the track record of the second generation is not great. Only a small group of us, like Jane Fonda, have succeeded.

\*

# THE VERY BEST OF KIRK DOUGLAS

Acting is a youthful profession.

*

I didn't start out to be a movie star. I started out to be an actor.

*

Virtue is not photogenic, so I liked playing bad guys. But, whenever I played a bad guy, I tried to find something good in him, and that kept my contact with the audience.

*

I didn't think I was so tough until I did 'Champion'; then I was a tough guy.

\*

People are always talking about the old days. They say that the old movies were better, that the old actors were so great. But I don't think so. All I can say about the old days is that they have passed.

\*

I have been an actor for most of my life. When I started out, I didn't think about anything except what was good for me. Like many movie stars, I became all wrapped up in myself.

\*

When I first came to Hollywood, the blacklist was just starting, and they were having hearings in Washington. What most people don't know is the judge of these hearings himself was later convicted of misappropriation.

## THE VERY BEST OF KIRK DOUGLAS

'Spartacus' helped break the blacklist, because Spartacus was a real character.

\*

It isn't a manly profession. It's a childish profession. You couldn't be a complete, grown-up adult and be an actor . . . I mean, if I were a sophisticated adult, how could I say, "Here I am, fighting evil, represented by Yul Brynner"? You have to have a childish part of you! It's true! You know, I watch as my kids have grown up, I've watched, them, you know. Children are natural actors; they pretend they're cops and robbers, and I think all actors retain a certain amount of that within themselves. They have to, or they can't function as actors. And that's why they become self-deprecating.

\*

I never had any desire to be a film actor. I never thought I was the good-looking movie type, which I assumed they wanted.

## DAVID GRAHAM

\*

Making movies is a form of narcissism.

\*

Acting is make-believe. I never believe I'm the character; I want you to believe.

\*

When you become a star, you don't change - everyone else does.

\*

It's tough to make a movie about movies... We're all too close to it. But 'The Bad and the Beautiful' was very good.

*

I've always believed virtue is not photogenic, and I think I've always been attracted to a part, uh, I'd rather play the *evil* character, most of the time, than the nice fella. And I think it really *bothered* my mother, because she would tell people, "You know, my son's not like that, he's really a nice boy!"

*

All children are natural actors, and I'm still a kid. If you grow up completely, you can never be an actor.

*

People are composed of many things, and in my work, what influences me is the complexity of people - the chiaroscuro of dark and light. When I play a strong guy, I try to find, where is he weak? And, conversely, when I play a weak guy, where is he strong?

*

The older you get, the more awards you get. So, if you live long enough, then you get all the awards eventually.

*

Speaking about *Paths of Glory*:

A truly great film with a truly great theme: the insanity and brutality of war. As I predicted, it made no money.

# 5 ABOUT OTHER CELEBRITIES

Linda Darnell is the most unspoilt star on the screen -- and also the most beautiful.

\*

About Anne Hathaway:

She's gorgeous! Wow! Where were you when I was making pictures?

\*

# DAVID GRAHAM

About John Wayne:

I did four movies with him. We were a strange combination. He was a Republican and I was a Democrat. We argued all the time.

\*

I love talking to interesting people - people like O.J. Simpson, Andretti... I love champions. A champion has something special about him.

\*

My first job was on Broadway. Then I went into the Navy. When I came out of the Navy, I went back to Broadway and a friend of mine, Lauren Bacall, was in Hollywood filming with Humphrey Bogart. She told one of her producers I was great in my play, and he saw it and cast me in 'The Strange Love of Martha Ivers'.

I've finally gotten away from Burt Lancaster. My luck has changed for the better. I've got nice-looking girls in my films now.

*

Speaking about Michael Moore (specifically his interview with Heston in *Bowling for Columbine*):

I cannot forgive the way he treated Charlton Heston. Even if I don't agree with much of Heston's politics, Chuck is a gentleman. He agreed to have an interview with Moore, and Moore took advantage of the situation and made Chuck look foolish. He had been invited to Heston's home and he was treated with courtesy. I winced when I saw the expression on Chuck's face change as he realized that he had been duped. And yet he remained a gentleman and dismissed the interloper with grace.

*

About Doris Day:

That face she shows the world -- smiling, only talking
good, happy, tuned into God -- as far as I'm concerned,
that's just a mask. I haven't a clue as to what's underneath.
Doris is just about the remotest person I know.

*

John Wayne was a great star. But he always played Wayne.
Anything else he didn't regard as manly. Now someone
like Burt Lancaster is just the opposite; the living proof
that you can be a sensitive actor and macho at the same
time.

*

Cancer does give you a new rejuvenation. I know what it's
like to be down. I lost a couple of good friends - Larry
Hagman and Nick Ashford - who had the same type of
cancer that I did, and that makes you think.

\*

Senator McCarthy was an awful man who was finding Communists all over the country. He blacklisted the writers who wouldn't obey his edict. The heads of the studios were hypocrites who went along with it. My company produced Spartacus, written by Dalton Trumbo, a blacklisted writer, under the name Sam Jackson. Too many people were using false names back then. I was embarrassed. I was young enough to be impulsive, so even though I was warned against it, I used his real name on the screen.

\*

John Wayne was a star because he always played John Wayne. Frankly, he wasn't an excellent actor, but good heavens, what a star! It wasn't John Wayne who served the roles; the roles served John Wayne.

\*

When he was asked who his favourite director was:

I would NEVER do that. I've enjoyed working with Wilder, Wyler, Mankiewicz. Hawks, Kazan. I did three films with Minelli and got nominated for two of them - but I could never name just one director.

*

Tony Curtis was one of the best-looking guys in Hollywood. He was often described as beautiful, but he was also a fine actor. I worked with Tony in "The Vikings" and in "Spartacus", and we were friends for a long time. What I will miss most about him is his sense of humor. It was always fun to be with him.

# 6 GENERAL PHILOSOPHY AND HUMOUR

Fame is as much about luck as it is about talent, perhaps more.

\*

In order to achieve anything you must be brave enough to fail.

\*

## DAVID GRAHAM

Why can't a woman be more like a dog, huh? So sweet, loving, attentive.

\*

You have to have a childish part of you! It's true!

\*

You must know how to function and how to maintain yourself and you must have a love of what you do.

\*

You know, you have to have some inner philosophy to deal with adversity.

\*

The learning process continues until the day you die.

\*

No matter how bad things are, they can always be worse.
So what if my stroke left me with a speech impediment?
Moses had one, and he did all right.

\*

Love has more depth as you get older.

\*

## DAVID GRAHAM

When you reach 95, after you get over your surprise, you start looking back.

\*

If you want to know about a man you can find out an awful lot by looking at who he married.

\*

Life is like a B-picture script! It is that corny. If I had my life story offered to me to film, I'd turn it down.

\*

Fear is a terrible thing. It makes you do awful things.

\*

If the good guy gets the girl, it's rated PG; If the bad guy gets the girl, it's rated R; and if everybody gets the girl, it's rated X.

\*

Sometimes, the thing that ties you down sets you free.

\*

Virtue is not photogenic. What is it to be a nice guy? To be nothing, that's what. A big fat zero with a smile for everybody.

\*

I think half the success in life comes from first trying to find out what you really want to do. And then going ahead and doing it.

\*

You have to leave your country to get a perspective, to see what makes America great. Now I can say that nowhere in the world is there a match for what we have in Hollywood.

\*

If you want to see a star, don't go to Hollywood. Come to Palm Springs.

# 7 AN OPEN LETTER TO THE YOUTH OF AMERICA

An open letter from Kirk Douglas to the youth of America, released in 2006:

My name is Kirk Douglas. You may know me. If you don't . . . Google me. I was a movie star and I'm Michael Douglas' dad, Catherine Zeta-Jones' father-in-law, and the grandparents of their two children. Today I celebrate my 90th birthday.

I have a message to convey to America's young people. A 90th birthday is special. In my case, this birthday is not only special but miraculous. I survived World War II, a helicopter crash, a stroke, and two new knees.

It's a tradition that when a "birthday boy" stands over his cake he makes a silent wish for his life and then blows out the candles. I have followed that tradition for 89 years but on my 90th birthday, I have decided to rebel. Instead of making a silent wish for myself, I want to make a loud wish for The World.

Let's face it: The World is in a mess and you are inheriting it. Generation Y, you are on the cusp. You are the group facing many problems: abject poverty, global warming, genocide, AIDS and suicide bombers, to name a few. These problems exist and the world is silent. We have done very little to solve these problems. Now we leave it to you. You have to fix it because the situation is intolerable.

You need to rebel, to speak up, write, vote, and care about people and the world you live in. We live in the best country in the world. I know. My parents were Russian immigrants. America is a country where EVERYONE, regardless of race, creed, or age has a chance. I had that chance. You are the generation that is most impacted and the generation that can make a difference.

I love this country because I came from a life of poverty. I was able to work my way through college and go into acting, the field that I love. There is no guarantee in this country that you will be successful. But you always have a chance. Nothing should interfere with it. You have to make sure that nothing stands in the way.

When I blow out my candles - 90! . . . it will take a long time . . . but I'll be thinking of you.

DAVID GRAHAM

## ABOUT THE AUTHOR

David Graham is a British author of a number of published articles and a film enthusiast. He currently lives in Paris with his wife, Janine, and two sons, James and George.

DAVID GRAHAM

Printed in Great Britain
by Amazon